Day1

GTD
Getting Things Done

Schedule

-Believe in yourself-

Day 2

GTD
Getting Things Done

Schedule

-Good for You-

Day3

GTD
Getting Things Done

Schedule

-Don't Worry, Be Happy-

Day4

GTD
Getting Things Done

Schedule

-You are not alone-

Day5

GTD
Getting Things Done

Schedule

-All the best for your future-

Day 6

GTD
Getting Things Done

Schedule

-With every good wish-

Day 7

GTD
Getting Things Done

Schedule

-Things will turn out fine-

Day8

GTD
Getting Things Done

Schedule

-Dreams come true-

Day 9

GTD
Getting Things Done

Schedule

-Live, Love, Laugh and be Happy!-

Day 10

GTD
Getting Things Done

Schedule

-Things will turn out fine-

Day 11

GTD
Getting Things Done

Schedule

-Let your success story begin-

Day12

GTD
Getting Things Done

Schedule

-Wishing you a future filled with happiness-

Day13

GTD
Getting Things Done

Schedule

-You're precious and treasured-

Day 14

GTD
Getting Things Done

Schedule

-I owe what I am now to you-

Day15

GTD
Getting Things Done

Schedule

-I'm always on your side-

Day16

GTD
Getting Things Done

Schedule

-Do one thing at a time, and do well-

Day17

GTD
Getting Things Done

Schedule

-Bad times make a good man-

Day 18

GTD
Getting Things Done

Schedule

=Journey of a thousand miles begins with single step=

Day19

GTD
Getting Things Done

Schedule

-I know that my future is not just a dream-

Day20

GTD
Getting Things Done

Schedule

-I will greet this day with love in my heart-

Day21

GTD
Getting Things Done

Schedule

-True mastery of any skill takes a lifetime-

Day 22

GTD
Getting Things Done

Schedule

-Where there is a will, there is a way-

Day 23

| GTD
Getting Things Done | Schedule |

-Victory belongs to the most persevering-

Day24

GTD
Getting Things Done

Schedule

-Nothing is impossible-

Day25

GTD
Getting Things Done

Schedule

-Winners do what losers don't want to do-

Day 26

GTD
Getting Things Done

Schedule

—Every noble work is at first impossible—

Day27

GTD
Getting Things Done

Schedule

—What a man needs most is appreciated—

Day28

GTD
Getting Things Done

Schedule

-The best preparation for tomorrow is doing your best today-

Day29

GTD
Getting Things Done

Schedule

-Those who turn back never reach the summit-

Day 30

GTD
Getting Things Done

Schedule

=Pursue your object; be it what it will; steadily and indefatigably=

Day31

GTD Getting Things Done	Schedule

-I will greet this day with love in my heart-

www.ingramcontent.com/pod-product-compliance
Lightning Source LLC
Chambersburg PA
CBHW051940210526
45473CB00006B/2318